HAWAIIAN QUILTS

Stella M. Jones

KU'U HAE ALOHA, (My Beloved Flag)
Made before 1918, cotton, red, white, blue, yellow.
Quilting: following the pattern, 91" x 91".
Lent by Mrs. James L. Murray, Maui.

HAWAIIAN QUILTS

Stella M. Jones

*Including a catalog of the exhibition,
"The Quilt — A Hawaiian Heritage," held at the
Honolulu Academy of Arts, October 13 - November 18, 1973*

*Published jointly by the Daughters of Hawaii,
Honolulu Academy of Arts and Mission Houses Museum,
Honolulu, Hawaii, 1973*

ORIGINALLY PUBLISHED IN 1930
BY THE HONOLULU ACADEMY OF ARTS, HONOLULU, HAWAII.
REVISED AND RESET EDITION, PUBLISHED JOINTLY
BY THE DAUGHTERS OF HAWAII, HONOLULU ACADEMY OF ARTS
AND MISSION HOUSES MUSEUM, HONOLULU, HAWAII, 1973

LIBRARY OF CONGRESS CATALOG CARD NO. 73-88714

COPYRIGHT 1973, HONOLULU ACADEMY OF ARTS
DESIGN, JOSEPH FEHER
PHOTOGRAPHY, RAYMOND SATO
PRINTED BY EDWARD ENTERPRISES, INC., HONOLULU, HAWAII, U.S.A.

INTRODUCTION TO THE SECOND EDITION

Here in Hawaii as across the United States people have been awakening to the values of traditional handcrafts. In an age when most things are mass-produced and disposable there is a new regard for the unique objects which are the creations of an artist's mind and hands.

For more than 150 years quilting as an art form and craft has been a cherished tradition in Hawaii, works being prized as family heirlooms by succeeding generations. Though the basic techniques of patchwork quilting were derived from New England examples, the style of the Hawaiian quilt evolved in the mid-19th century through the adaptation to appliqued quilting of a red-on-white *kapa* pattern. Today the craft is still employed as a medium of expression, with new designs and materials being introduced.

Such is the current interest in Hawaiian quilting here and elsewhere that it has prompted a republication of the noted monograph by Stella M. Jones, first published by the Honolulu Academy of Arts at the time of a quilt exhibition in 1930 and long out of print. The collaborative efforts of the Daughters of Hawaii and the Mission Houses Museum with the Academy have resulted in this more elaborate and larger second edition. As the definitive work on the subject, the three organizations take pleasure in jointly making *Hawaiian Quilts* again available to the public.

Stella May Jones is best remembered in Hawaii as the author of this work. Little is known of her personal life. She was born in St. Mary-of-the-Woods, Indiana in 1887 and attended the University of Chicago, Northwestern University and the Graduate School, Yale University.

Stella Jones served the Bernice P. Bishop Museum, Honolulu, in various capacities for many years. She was secretary to the director, Dr. Herbert Ernest Gregory, assisted Dr. E. S. Craighill Handy, Ethnologist, in projects pertaining to Hawaiian culture and was editor of museum publications. Her study, "Economic Adjustment of Hawaiians to European Culture," published in *Pacific Affairs* in 1931, reflects her considerable knowledge of early crafts in the Islands. In the years following the publication of *Hawaiian Quilts* she was a frequent lecturer at the Honolulu Academy of Arts. She died in Honolulu in 1971.

The quilts selected for our current exhibition, which in part celebrates the reissuing of Stella M. Jones's book, were made during the historical period that ended with the death of Queen Liliuokalani in 1917. Selections have been based primarily on aesthetic qualities that would ensure a harmonious presentation of the quilt as an art form of unique character within the Hawaiian heritage.

At this time the three participating institutions are establishing a documentary file on Hawaiian quilts made prior to 1940. This permanent record will be housed at the Academy and will be available for scholarly research only. Every effort will be made to prevent the copying of designs represented in the file just as they were protected by an unwritten code of ethics in the Monarchy Period and later. By the same token, *the public is earnestly requested not to borrow patterns from the quilts illustrated in this publication* but to create their own original designs, thus perpetuating rather than violating the spirit of Hawaiian quilt-making.

MARY HELEN GAY STYAN, Regent
DAUGHTERS OF HAWAII

JAMES W. FOSTER, Director
HONOLULU ACADEMY OF ARTS

RICHARD L. BYARD, Director
MISSION HOUSES MUSEUM

Honolulu, Hawaii, October, 1973

In republishing this monograph it was necessary to make some minor changes in the text. In light of current knowledge, several factual errors have been corrected. Also, the author's references in 1930 to times past have been updated.

Preface

Any study that leads to contact with the Hawaiian people is rich in experiences. The preparation of this small work has introduced me into many kinds of homes, homes where kahilis and calabashes of the old alii blend with the best of modern furnishings and humble homes where the bed is still made Hawaiian-fashion upon the floor. But whether swept with a vacuum cleaner or a broom of coconut midribs, all of them were scrupulously clean and tidy.

Hawaiian quilters look upon their work seriously, even reverently, reflecting perhaps the attitude of earlier days toward craftsmanship. A woman who had been nursing her small daughter through a long illness was dozing beside the bed one night when the vague idea of a quilt design came to her unsought. During the next three days the details became clear in her mind, and she procured the material and worked upon the quilt during the little girl's convalescence. Upon completion, the quilt was presented to her daughter.

Another woman related that as a girl of seventeen in a country district she came to love a young Chinese of the neighborhood. Her parents opposed the match, insisting that she marry a Hawaiian.

When at last the mother consented she declared that none of the calabashes nor other heirlooms should be taken to another race nor was the daughter to have any of the quilts that had been intended for her. The couple moved to Honolulu. The young wife was ashamed before the other women because she had no quilt for her bed. She purchased the necessary material but had no pattern and was too humiliated to ask for one. Then one night as she lay asleep she dreamed a pattern. The dream was so vivid that it awakened her and, rising, she cut the design direct from the material and basted it upon the background before going back to sleep. In the morning she was delighted with her handwork. A friend who helped her finish the quilt named it *Ka La'i o Pua* (The Calm of Pua Lane).

This study of Hawaiian quilts was fostered by the Honolulu Academy of Arts. It includes information gathered by others interested in the subject, particularly Mrs. Alva E. Steadman and Mrs. Joseph R. Farrington. In addition to those whose quilts are reproduced here I am indebted for information to Mrs. Percy E. Deverill, Mrs. E. Lahilahi Webb, Mrs. C. Montague Cooke, Jr., Mrs. J. K. Smythe, Mrs. H. F. Bertelman, Mrs. Mia and, on Kauai, Mrs. Lota and Mrs. Kaaiawi. We are also indebted to the many who have generously loaned their quilts for exhibitions at the Academy.

GARDEN ISLAND
Kauai has long been known as the Garden Island because of the luxuriance of its vegetation, a sobriquet further earned by the planting of miles of roadside with flowering shrubs and plants. The establishment of a weekly newspaper, The Garden Island, in 1904 was the inspiration of this pattern, fittingly worked out in floral design
Originally bright blue on white
Owned by Mrs. Dora Isenberg, Kauai

S.M.J.

MANU LAWE LEKA
(The Carrier Pigeon)
The carrier pigeon was introduced
into the Islands when the United
States Army was stationed on
Oahu and tested this means of
communication between the islands.
The pigeon with a letter in its
beak is the motif of a quilt pattern
said to commemorate the
beginning of regular mail service
to Kauai
Light blue on white
Owned by Mrs. Dora Isenberg,
Kauai

NA LEI MAMO
The feather of the extinct
mamo bird, the prerogative of the
alii and in the old days used
only in cloaks, helmets and leis,
is the subject of this quilt
executed in pale green on buff
Collection of the Honolulu
Academy of Arts

HAWAIIAN QUILTS

THE BIRD OF PARADISE
The theme of this quilt is the faithless lover. Forming a border are sprays of green leaves and red flowers representing ohia lehua trees, on each of which is lightly perched a bird, presumably the mamo. A wreath of the flowers enclosing figures of the bird in flight forms the medallion. The designer generously represents her lover turning from sweetheart to sweetheart as naturally as the forest bird flits from one flowering tree to another.

THE BEGINNING

On Monday morning, April 3, 1820, the American Board of Missions held its first sewing circle in the Sandwich Islands. The place of meeting was the brig Thaddeus, one hundred and sixty-two days out of Boston, as, almost at her journey's end, she sailed along the western coast of Hawaii after a brief stop at Kawaihae.

A group of eleven women were seated on lauhala mats on deck: Kalakua, queen dowager; Namahana, her sister and also widow of Kamehameha I; two wives of chief Kalanimoku, their ample figures wrapped in folds of tapa from waist to below the knees, their brown bosoms and shoulders bare; and seven young New England matrons, wives of the first missionaries to these islands. Lucy Thurston, Lucia Holman, Sybil Bingham, Nancy Ruggles, Mercy Whitney, Jerusha Chamberlain and Mrs. Elisha Loomis were dressed in the tight-waisted, tight-sleeved garments of the day, their ankles no doubt tucked discreetly beneath their billowing skirts.

Mrs. Thurston later wrote, "Kalakua, queen dowager, was directress ... Mrs. Holman and Mrs. Ruggles were executive officers, to ply the scissors and prepare the work. The four women of rank were furnished with calico patchwork to sew, a new employment to them."

The Easterners had picked up only a few Hawaiian expressions from the four native boys travelling with their party, the Hawaiian women had learned very little English, but scissors, cloth, needles and thread have their own language and the sewing party progressed happily. It is recorded that a dress for Kalakua was cut out "... in the fashion of 1819 ..." which, woman-like, she wanted finished to wear ashore at Kailua.

That these young women, naturally quite curious to see their new home along whose strange and beautiful shore they were then passing, could so occupy themselves is a tribute to their remarkable self-discipline and devotion.

Whether the patchwork thus begun ever grew into a quilt is not recorded nor is the date the Hawaiians forsook the simple blocked patterns of their teachers and gave their fancies free rein in the glorious handwork that is now known as the Hawaiian quilt.

The patchwork blocks of the early eighteen hundreds in

New England were made from bits of cloth, almost invariably blue and white, green and white or black and white printed calico combined with plain white, but otherwise they bear little relation to the Hawaiian quilt.

Some resemblance can be noted between the Hawaiian quilt and the applique patterns of later and more prosperous days in America, particularly quilts of the South and the Middle West made about 1840, but the Island patterns are much less sophisticated and the manner of cutting is unique. Before quilting the design is flat, rarely embodying more than one color on white, the balance being maintained through exact repetition of motif. Its primary motivation is expression rather than ornamentation. In its imagery and method of expression the Hawaiian quilt ranks as a distinct type of needlework.

NATIVE BEDDING

Though the use of needle and thread was an innovation to Hawaiian women, the making of gracious bedding was not ". . . a new employment to them." Like most Polynesians, the Hawaiians were fastidious about their bedding. They spread upon the stone floor layer upon layer of coarse mats in place of bedsteads. A pile of mats of finer weave constituted the mattress. The higher the rank of the occupants the finer the texture of the mats and the higher the beds. Tapas were used as coverlets only.

Throughout Hawaii mats were woven from *lauhala*, the ribbon-like leaves of the pandanus. Kauai and Niihau were famed for their mats of flax *(makaloa)*, so soft and fine as to have the appearance of silk. Kawelo, a warrior of prehistoric Hawaii, urged his wife to dispose of his adversary, Kauahoa, of Kauai,

*"When Hanalei thou shalt possess,
And the mats of Niihau thou shalt wear,
And the birds of Kaula thou shalt eat."*

In the same account Kawelo makes advances to a native chief of Kauai:

*"Say, Aikanaka, chief of this height,
Who lives on the hill of Nounou,
Come and let us make friends,
When we will together take possession of Kauai,
And sleep on the mats."*

The Hawaiian women had long been skillful in handling the wet inner bark of the wauke plant and in shaping it into sheets of tapa of uniform size and thickness. They were accustomed, too, to decorate this white surface with various designs of many colors and were clever in building up their patterns bit by bit with the aid of the small stencils that they dipped into their native dyes and pressed upon the tapa.

Though poorer families were forced to content themselves with less, a proper set of bed tapas consisted of four large white sheets topped by a stamped tapa, all fastened together at the foot. This is called a *pa'u o Lu'ukia*, or robe of a legendary woman, Lu'ukia, who is said to have come to Hawaii from New Zealand wearing four white tapas beneath one of beautiful color and design.[1] Bedding was kept clean by washing with a damp cloth and by frequent sunning. When not in use it was kept in rolls across the rafters of the house and made fragrant with bits of sandalwood or seeds of the *mokihana*.

THE DEVELOPMENT

During those first busy years of adjustment, instruction in sewing seems to have been desultory if, indeed, it had any place at all in the crowded program of the missionary schools. Several accounts exist telling of the struggle the missionary wives had in doing the sewing for their own families as well as for the royal rulers, who made demands for dresses of silk and for ruffled shirts.

But in 1828 Maria Ogden, a maiden woman of retiring disposition "... (who) accomplished a vast amount of work in a most unobstrusive manner ...," arrived to devote her full time to instructing Hawaiian girls in domestic arts and to nursing the sick. The first year she was stationed on Kauai, then at Lahainaluna, Maui. In 1838 Miss Ogden began her twenty years of service in the boarding school for girls at Wailuku, Maui where "... forty-two little girls spent two hours daily in braiding, sewing, washing, ironing and mending their own clothes ..."

In 1836 Lydia Brown from New Hampshire joined the missionary group to teach domestic industries. Spinning cotton, carding, weaving wool[2] and sewing were emphasized as studies. During her twenty-nine years of service she taught on Maui, Hawaii and Oahu.

No direct mention of quiltmaking is made in the records of the activities of these women, but it is reasonable to expect that the little Hawaiian girls were given bits of cloth for

LILIA O KE AWAWA
(Lily of the Valley)
White on pink

---

[1] I have seen many *pa'u o Lu'ukia* folded away with Hawaiian quilts, and on chilly nights they are still put into service by the older Hawaiians.

[2] The sheep from which the wool was sheared were doubtless descendants of the ewes and rams left by Vancouver in 1791-1794.

LILY
Red on white
Owned by Mrs. H. E. A. Castle

KAOMI MALIE
(Press Gently) Red on white
Collection of the
Honolulu Academy of Arts

piecework, following the New England custom under which their instructors had been reared. Miss Brown notes that the Hawaiians adopted the needle and thread "... with surprising aptitude ..."

Later recruits to the mission service brought more patchwork quilts from New England. A letter sent from the Sandwich Islands Mission to Boston in 1822 recounted, "We received from the Board by this conveyance (the schooner Rover) a box, ... and, with the rest, a bedquilt from the young ladies in Miss E. Dewey's school, Blanford, for Kaahumanu, which was very acceptable to this honored female ruler."

In 1830 Mrs. Laura Fish Judd received from the East "friendship blocks," each bearing in outline stitch a quotation from the Bible and the name of the donor.

The missionary barrels, which took an entire year to travel by freighter from Boston around Cape Horn, contained — among the clothing, sacks of flour and sugar — patchpieces which were later distributed to the Hawaiian women as they sat on the ground under the trees at their quilting bees. Patchwork quilts were made, too, at the missionary boarding school for girls at Koloa, Kauai. On Oahu, the Lima Kokua Society of young Hawaiian girls made a pieced quilt which they sent to the Bingham family, then conducting a mission station in the Gilbert Islands (1858-1868). About 1845 Princess Pauahi, later Mrs. Charles Reed Bishop, made at the Royal School, under the tutelage of Mrs. Amos Cooke, a most elaborate and beautiful quilt of silk patchwork.

But in the old Hawaiian homes there were no scrap bags, for the holokus were cut full and straight, taking the full width of the cloth and leaving little for quilt pieces. Cloth received as samples at the local dry goods stores were begged for the purpose.

But money was fairly plentiful at the time and colorful calicoes were to be had at the stores, as were large, seamless sheets. To cut new materials into bits to be sewn together seemed a futile waste of time. It was quite natural, therefore, that these women, accustomed each to her own design on her tapa beater and to her own individual woodblocked patterns, should produce patterns of their own.

A woman who was a retainer of Kamehameha IV and Queen Emma was of the opinion that the Hawaiian method originated upon the birth of the Prince of Hawaii (1858), when the women began making quilts for the heir apparent. She said that on his first birthday a processional was held and the quilts were presented to the little prince. It is quite natural that on such an occasion the Hawaiians would turn to a more colorful and individualistic medium for expressing their joy than was afforded by the patchwork quilt.

Other informants, however, say that the method originated on Maui, traceable, perhaps, to the efforts of Miss Ogden and Miss Brown.

The Hawaiian type of quilt has long been made on each of the inhabited Hawaiian islands. On Kauai and Maui quilt-making is still actively carried on, as it is to a considerable extent on Hawaii. On Oahu the art, which was more or less dying out due to a scarcity of quilters (there were many to design and applique but few with the patience and the time to do the actual quilting) has been revitalized, attracting an increasing number of needleworkers.

Though many of the old collections are scattered among the boys and girls as they marry or go to boarding school, most of the old Hawaiian families have some treasured quilts. The old ones, of course, have disappeared through use but some known to be over a hundred years old may still be in existence. The older patterns show a marked tendency to simpler design and less contrasting material and all are made of turkey red on white, which would seem to establish the *pa'i'ula* (tapa) as the original conception. So far as observed there are no distinguishing characteristics on the different islands except for a quilting stitch said to belong to Kauai.

KUKUI LANIKAULA
This quilt was named for a well-known kukui grove on northeastern Molokai. About 1650 the King of Maui determined to invade the island of Hawaii and the priests were given to understand that all auguries concerning the project were expected to be favorable. Lanikaula of Molokai was the only kahuna with sufficient courage to prophesy against the foolhardy undertaking. The King was angry with him and replied, "When I return I will burn you alive." The Maui army was defeated on Hawaii and the King killed. Upon his death Lanikaula was buried in the great kukui grove which was then named in his honor.

TECHNIQUE

The material is first washed to make sure of fast color and uniform shrinkage. If that for the background and lining is not of one piece it is seamed lengthwise. The most common style, a square design with unbroken or slightly broken border, is cut from material folded diaper-wise, eightfold, the creases forming the corners of the border, the necessary seams falling at the middle of the sides. Thus by cutting one motif the entire border is produced at one time and with exact repetition of the motif. This leaves a large, roughly circular piece for the medallion, which also is cut folded. Some women design freehand with the scissors, others cut the pattern first in paper. In the old days tapa was used for this purpose. Both border and medallion are then basted on the background.

This much accomplished, the quilt can be used as pickup work and the design appliqued at leisure.

In another style of pattern a motif is cut the entire length of the folded material, producing four repetitions which radiate from the center of the quilt to the corners.

Wool only was used for padding the earlier quilts, prepared

QUILTING DESIGNS: *1, 2, parallel lines; 3, diagonal squares; 4, 5, 8, 9, blocks perhaps taken from blocks of patchwork design; 6, honu ipu (turtle's back) said to belong to Kauai; 7, shell pattern.*

as taught by Lydia Brown. The wool was first cleaned, bleached and carded (the cards were made of wire stuck into leather which was mounted on wood and they had handles), then the wool was brushed back and forth and made into squares, held up to the light to make sure of even thickness. The backing, or lining, of the quilt was laid out flat and evenly covered with the wool. The decorated top was placed over the wool and the whole tacked together. Wool batting and cotton batting have replaced the homemade padding.

Just as much of the quilt as could be worked upon at a time was exposed, with the rest kept rolled up in the manner of New England. The "horses" for the quilting frames were made in two sizes, high ones for the missionary ladies, who used chairs, and low ones for the Hawaiian women, who sat on the ground. In oldtime Hawaii the actual quilting was done at bees, as in New England, the Hawaiian women going from house to house of their friends for this labor of love.

In later years too many hands were avoided, and nowadays quilting done by one person only is preferred, insuring uniform stitches.

The Hawaiian women at first used parallel lines and diagonal squares in the quilting of their applique patterns, in the manner of the patchwork quilts, marking them in advance with pencil or chalked string. Later they improved upon their more elaborate quilts by following the pattern in freehand quilting; that is, they stitched a series of lines within and without, and parallel to, the outlines of the design, the interspaces filled with graceful scrolls. Some quilts combine a general following-the-pattern technique with a diagonal quilting pattern about a plain border. Wool padding naturally gives the softer and deeper hillock between stitches, called *kulipu'u* (lump hill) and shows off the quilting to better advantage than does cotton.

ETHICS

A fairly well-defined code of ethics prevails as to the use of quilt designs or patterns. The originator of a design names it, and that design and that name are held inseparable. Exchange of patterns has always been held a bond of close friendship. While another to whom the pattern has been given can alter the design to suit her taste, introducing new elements and changing the proportions, the name prevails so long as the general outline is retained. Color can be changed without thought, though some designs naturally imply the use of certain colors.

Patterns are known to have been stolen even from the

clothesline where the quilts had been hung to dry or to air, for some women, very clever with the scissors, could stand far off and cut the pattern by sight. The originator of a particularly well-loved pattern wisely kept it secret until the coverlet was quilted, thereby establishing her undisputable claim.

The owner of a design, upon finding it strayed from home, might compose a song slyly making reference to the quilt, which would greatly embarrass the stealer. It is well, therefore, in cutting a pattern obtained surreptitiously to alter the design sufficiently to make a brave claim for originality.

KUKUI LANIKAULA *(detail)*
showing the manner of quilting
by following the pattern.
Mrs. Kehele, Kauai

QUILT DESIGNS

To one unfamiliar with Hawaii no doubt many of these quilt names and their designs will appear farfetched. This is due not to lack of logic on the part of the designers but to the difficulty of interpreting in English the allegorical thought of the Hawaiian and the subtlety of her expression. Then, too, there is not necessarily any connection between the actual design and the theme. Many a woman, having worked out in her quilt some meaning known only to herself, gives it a name foreign to the subject and keeps the interpretation secret.

Nor are all quilts symbolic, for any new design or subject that strikes the fancy may be reproduced on a quilt. The chandelier in the Palace when it was new was a favorite subject. The highly elaborate design in a stained glass window of the first parlor car in Hawaii was another. A vase or a basket of flowers in the house or any design seen in cloth or embroidery may be used.

NA LEI MOKIHANA
(The Mokihana leis)
The mokihana is a small tree
growing in a few places on Kauai.
Leis of its seed are valued for
their lasting fragrance
Lavender on buff / Owned by
Mrs. Montgomery, Lihue, Kauai

Any classification of Hawaiian quilt designs must, of course, be arbitrary. On the basis of theme, however, the following may be found acceptable and convenient: quilts with naturalistic motif, those associated with a place and those with historical themes. Such patterns as Pile of Lumber, Press Gently or the saw pattern, however, defy classification.

The Hawaiian woman drew upon her garden for many of her designs. The actual leaves of the breadfruit, of the pumpkin and papaya, fig leaves and ferns she used as patterns. The widespread tentacles of the octopus, the outlines of the turtle and *Mahina* (The Crescent Moon) were very oldtime themes for quilt patterns.

With the naturalistic designs also may be included *Lilia o ke Awawa* (Lily of the Valley); fuchsia pattern; *Lilia o Sepania Kepani* (Japanese Lily); *Ka U'i o Amerika* (The

13

KA MAKANI KA'ILI ALOHA
Winds, to the Polynesians, had definite personalities and are named according to their characteristics. This quilt has been named for a gentle breeze, Ka Makani Ka'ili Aloha, the wind that wafts love from one to another / Made by Ninia, the mother of Mrs. Elizabeth Kahookano, Waikiki, Honolulu

KA U'I O MAUI
(The Beauty of Maui)
Red on white
Made by Mrs. Kehele, Kauai

Beauty of America); pineapple pattern in many designs; *poni-mo'i* (carnation); grapevine; *ohelo* berries; hibiscus flowers; *panini* (prickly pear); *Pika Pua Waiohinu* (Pitcher of Dahlias); and *Popo Lehua* (Round Ball of Lehua Blossoms).

The *lei*, or garland, which has so important a place in life in Hawaii is amply represented in quilts: *Lei Mamo* (*Lei* of the Feathers of the *Mamo* Bird); *Lei Loke* (Rose Wreath); *Lei o May* (*Lei* of May); *Lei ana ka U'i o ka Mokihana* (Wreathed in the Beauty of *Mokihana*); and *Lei o Hawaii*.

The striking beauty of a place, often associated with some event that had transpired there, is the inspiration for a large number of quilt designs. *Na Molokama*, the name of a waterfall at Hanalei, is strikingly adapted to a quilt pattern. Executed in cool green on white, it is designed to give the impression of looking upon tumbling waters through the green ferns growing along the sides. In the center is an irregular circle of white representing a pool into which flow straight waterways from each corner of the quilt, fresh, uncoiled fern fronds forming the pattern.

Kuahiwi Nani o Haleakala (The Beautiful Mountain of Haleakala) is a flower design arranged about a center representing the crater. *Kai Holu o Kahului* (Rippling Sea of Kahului) represents the gentle rising and falling of the waves at Kahului. The watery mists of Eleile, Maui *Ka Uhiwai o Eleile* are portrayed in a famous quilt pattern which so far has not been located.

Rain on Kauai, Rain on Maui and *Ka U'i o Maui* (The Beauty of Maui) are graceful designs in red on white. *Ulu Kukui Lanikaula* (Kukui Grove of Lanikaula) commemorates a noted *kukui* grove on Molokai. Appreciation for hospitality received at *Na Laie Lua a ka Manu* was the inspiration of a quilt given that name.

A delicate design made over seventy-five years ago is named *Lihiwai o Kanaha* (Banks of Kanaha) and refers to a now long-dry stream *mauka* (toward the mountain) of Waikiki. An exquisite green pattern on a white background is named *Pahapaha o Polihale* (Seaweed at Polihale). Equally delicate is Watery Mists of Pu'uko *(Uhiwai o Pu'uko)*. *Ka Makani Ka'ili Aloha o Kipahulu* (The Kipahulu Wind that Steals Love) is said to have been stolen and renamed, originally being The Rain that Makes Noise on the House, so called by one who was sleeping in the new Palace before the roof was completed when sheet iron was used as a makeshift until more material arrived. The rain, falling upon the iron, disturbed the sleeper.

The days of old Hawaii are recalled by the theme of a quilt

which relates that in travelling upper Nuuanu Valley toward the *Pali* should it rain one could remove one's *holoku* and, wrapping it in a tight bundle, hold it behind one; in coming down the valley it could be held in the front, thus assuring dry garments at either end of the journey.

Some episode in the life of the quilter is often taken as the theme for a design, such as the graceful Garden Island pattern inspired by the printing of a weekly paper of that name on Kauai, and *Manu Lawe Leka* (The Carrier Pigeon), said to commemorate the beginning of regular mail service to the island of Kauai. In the quilt named The Bird of Paradise the theme of the faithless lover has an unusual and unconventional interpretation.

Religious enthusiasm inspired The Garden of Religious Light. The Biblical story of Adam and Eve in the Garden of Eden is graphically portrayed in an unusually fine piece of needlework.

Pride in her islands upon the discovery of pearls in Hawaii so stirred the heart of one woman that she composed an exquisite quilt which she named The Pearl of the Pacific.

Close friends often designed quilts for one another. Patterns were dedicated to a person as a mark of respect or love, as a book or poem is dedicated by the author. Designs without number were dedicated to the beloved Queen Liliuokalani. Shortly after her accession to the throne she made a tour of all the islands, as was the custom in Hawaii. On Niihau she remarked how close the breadfruit grew to the coral reef, whereupon a chant was composed including the line, *"Ulu hua i ka hapapa."* A quilt designed to commemorate the remark is so named. Another design symbolizes her handsome appearance, *Ka Lei o Ulumahiehie.*

At the time of the overthrow of the Hawaiian monarchy a quilt served a peculiar and touching function. During Queen Liliuokalani's detention in the Palace some of her close friends went into voluntary imprisonment with her and to pass the weary hours began a quilt of silk patchwork which quickly grew into a "love quilt." Blocks of rich materials easily associated with the donor, some of them embroidered with the name of the giver, were received. Thus her former subjects declared their love and continued loyalty to their Queen. Liliuokalani is said to have herself made one of the blocks.

Quilts were used also to perpetuate knowledge of the royal family of Hawaii, as in *Lei o Kaahumanu*, embodying Kaahumanu's crown, *kahili* and *lei*, and The *Kahili* and Fan of Kapiolani. The silver wreath *(lau kala)* on the dime of Kalakaua issue is a favorite element in historical designs, in

NA LA'IE LUA A KA MANU
This quilt, a gift to a hostess as an expression of appreciation for hospitality, is named for the place in which the designer was entertained. Two wreaths of flowers symbolize the two winds which daily blow about it, a calm wind and a boisterous one, as the name implies. The medallion repeats the design of a tapestry in the home
Red on white
Designed by Mrs. Jacobs, Kaimuki, Honolulu

GARDEN OF RELIGIOUS LIGHT
The joy experienced upon conversion to the Christian faith inspired this colorful design, which consists of orange colored fruit, red flowers and green foliage on a white background in a most cheerful combination
Designed by Mrs. Jacobs, Kaimuki, Honolulu

one quilt being combined with the comb of the Princess Kaiulani, *Ke Kahi o Kaiulani* (The Comb of Kaiulani).

The bungalow of Kalakaua which stood at the corner of Richards and Hotel streets is commemorated in a beautiful pink and white quilt called *Hale 'Akala o Kalakaua* (The Pink House of Kalakaua), the design of the cornice being reproduced in the quilt. *Pua o Ainahau* (Flowers of Aina-hau) recalls the time when the Waikiki section known as Ainahau contained the lovely home of Princess Kaiulani.

The most loved design, however, is *Ku'u Hae Aloha* (My Beloved Flag). Upon abdication of the Queen and the consequent lowering of their flag many of the Hawaiian people feared that they would not again be permitted to fly the emblem of their kingdom. They turned to the quilt as a means of perpetuating the flag and the coat-of-arms, and the result was My Beloved Flag, a design held so sacred as never to be put to common use.

Stella M. Jones

16

NA KALAUNU ME KA LEI MAILE, (Crowns and Maile Lei)
Made for Dr. Robert B. Williams, ca. 1880, Hawaii, cotton, green on white. Quilting: following the pattern, 72½″ x 68½″. Collection of Daughters of Hawaii.

18

Catalog

THE QUILT — A HAWAIIAN HERITAGE

An Exhibition, October 13-November 18, 1973,
at the Honolulu Academy of Arts.
Co-sponsored by the Daughters of Hawaii,
Honolulu Academy of Arts
and Mission Houses Museum.

Acknowledgements

This publication is made possible by the generous contributions of various business firms and individuals who are dedicated to the preservation of Hawaii's heritage. The sponsoring institutions express grateful thanks for their helpful participation.

The three sponsoring organizations are deeply grateful to the lenders to the exhibition whose names appear in the catalog portion of this publication. Their generosity in sharing these treasures with the public can only be fully appreciated in the Islands where old quilts have long been venerated as foremost among family heirlooms.

A warm expression of gratitude is offered those who most helpfully assisted in locating quilts throughout the State for a documentary file from which selections were made for this exhibition: Dora Jane Cole, Dora C. Derby, Robert A. Gahran, Josephine Leimalama Kamakau, Virginia Dominis Koch, Elizabeth F. Rice, Helen Kinau Wight Weeks and Gwendolyn G. M. Williams.

Sincere appreciation for their editing assistance is expressed to Barbara W. Prock, Honolulu Academy of Arts; Ilima Piianaia McGill; Agnes Conrad, Archivist, and Frances Frazier, Hawaiian Translator, Archives of Hawaii.

To those members of the Academy staff who have contributed in many ways to this project notably Marvell A. Hart, James H. Furstenberg, Robert Van Der Wege, Nancy T. Long and Fujio Kaneko, warmest thanks are extended.

Finally, special acknowledgement and gratitude are owing to Selden Washington, Assistant Director of the Academy, who served as the able and willing Coordinator of this endeavor, and to Joseph Feher, the Academy's Curator of Graphic Arts and Hawaiiana specialist, who was instrumental in many ways to the realization of both the exhibition and the publication.

TITLE UNKNOWN
Made ca. 1880, probably Maui, cotton, red on white. Quilting:
following the pattern, 82" x 81".
Collection of Kauai Museum.

CROSS AND WREATH
*Made for the Rev. Lorenzo Lyons, 1882, Hawaii, broadcloth on birdseye
cotton, pink, green, white. Quilting: diagonal squares, 81" x 72½".
Collection of Hawaiian Mission Children's Society, Oahu.*

NA KALAUNU ME NA KAHILI, (Crowns and Kahilis)
Made for the Parker family, 1890, Hawaii, percale, yellow on white.
Quilting: following the pattern, 80" x 58".
Lent by Mr. Richard Smart, Hawaii.

LILIA, (Lily)
Made by patients for Dr. Wood, 1895, cotton, white on red.
Quilting: following the pattern, 81" x 78½".
Collection of Daughters of Hawaii.

24

KU'U HAE ALOHA, (My Beloved Flag)
Made as a wedding present for Mrs. Harry A. Baldwin, 1897, Maui,
percale, red, white, blue. Quilting: following the pattern, 75" x 79".
Lent by Mrs. J. Walter Cameron, Maui.

LEI MAMO, (Mamo Lei)
*Probably made for a member of the Brickwood family, late 19th
century, cotton, red on white. Quilting: following the pattern,
parallel lines, 80" x 80".*
Collection of Honolulu Academy of Arts.

NA KALAUNU ME NA KAHILI, (Crowns and Kahilis)
Probably made by "Mother Rice" (Mrs. William Harrison Rice), 1886,
Kauai, cotton, red on white. Quilting: following the pattern, 75" x 75".
Lent by Mrs. Thomas D. King, Jr., Oahu.

NA KALAUNU, NA KAHILI ME NA PE'AHI,
(Crowns, Kahilis and Fans)
Made for Samuel Parker, 1897, Hawaii, percale, red on white.
Quilting: following the pattern, 96" x 85".
Lent by Mr. Richard Smart, Hawaii.

KA 'ULU, (Breadfruit)
Made for a member of the Brickwood family before 1900, cotton,
yellow on red. Quilting: following the pattern, 83" x 78".
Collection of Honolulu Academy of Arts.

KU'U HAE ALOHA, (My Beloved Flag)
Probably made ca. 1900, cotton, red, white, blue.
Quilting: following the pattern and diagonal blocks, 79″ x 74″.
Collection of Hawaii Mission Children's Society, Oahu.

TITLE UNKNOWN
Made by Mrs. Fanny Haia and Mrs. Helen Apa for Dr. Daes' wife, 1900,
Maui, cotton, lavender on white. Quilting: following the pattern,
96" x 96".
Lent by Mrs. John Hanchett, Maui.

HALA 'AI, (Pineapple)
Made for Mrs. Harry A. Baldwin, ca. 1900, Maui, cotton, maroon,
blue, white. Quilting: diagonal squares, 82" x 78".
Lent by Mrs. J. Walter Cameron, Maui.

32

AMERICAN EAGLE AND BUFFALO
Designed by William Malina to commemorate his trip across the
United States; made by Mrs. William Richmond, ca. 1900, Kauai,
cotton, red on white. Quilting: following the pattern, 85" x 81".
Lent by Mrs. Juliette Rice Wichman, Kauai.

TITLE UNKNOWN
Made for Mrs. Harry A. Baldwin, ca. 1900, Maui, cotton, blue on
white. Quilting: following the pattern, 82" x 78".
Lent by Mrs. J. Walter Cameron, Maui.

34

PUA NANA LA, (Sunflowers)
Made ca. 1900, Maui, cotton, orange on white. Quilting: following
the pattern, 88" x 80".
Lent by Mr. L. T. Cannon, Kauai.

LEI MAMO, (Mamo Lei)
Made for William K. McKee, Sr., ca. 1900, Hawaii, cotton, red on
white. Quilting: blocks, parallel lines, 91" x 84".
36
Lent by Mrs. William K. McKee, Sr., Oahu.

AMERICAN FLAG
Made after 1906, cotton, red, white, blue, green, yellow.
Quilting: following the pattern, 84" x 83¾".
Collection of Daughters of Hawaii.

KE KALAUNU, ME KA LEI, (Crown and Wreath)
*Made ca. 1900, cotton, yellow on red. Quilting: following the
pattern, 78¼" x 77¼".*
Collection of Daughters of Hawaii.

KA MOKUPUNI KIHAPAI, (The Garden Island)
Made by Mrs. Mahikoa for Mrs. Dora R. Isenberg, 1904, Kauai, cotton,
red on white. Quilting: following the pattern, 78" x 68".
Collection of Kauai Museum.

KU'U HAE ALOHA, (My Beloved Flag)
*Made ca. 1905, cotton, red, white, blue, yellow. Quilting: diagonal
lines and squares, 79½″ x 77½″.*
Collection of Daughters of Hawaii.

LEI LOKELANI, (Wreath of Roses)
Made for member of Parker family, 1910, Hawaii, percale, rose on
white. Quilting: following the pattern, 77" x 66".
Lent by Mr. Richard Smart, Hawaii.

KA U'I O MAUI, (The Beauty of Maui)
Design originated by Mrs. David Kamaiopili; made by Mrs. Kamakee
Paki Saffery, Maui, 1910, percale, red on white.
Quilting: following the pattern, 90" x 90".
Lent by Mrs. Winnifred S. Sanborn, Maui.

MELIA, (Plumeria)
Made by Mrs. Mary R. Medinos for her daughter Mary, ca. 1910, Maui,
cotton, green, rose, white. Quilting: following the pattern, 90" x 89".
Lent by Mrs. Rosalie L. Kehona, Maui.

KU'U HAE ALOHA, (My Beloved Flag)
*Made by Mrs. Crozier, ca. 1907, Maui, cotton, red, white, blue,
yellow. Quilting: following the pattern and parallel lines, 80″ x 79″.
Lent by Mr. L. T. Cannon, Kauai.*

KA 'ULU, (Breadfruit)
Made by Mrs. Mary R. Medinos for her children, ca. 1910, Maui,
cotton, green on white. Quilting: following the pattern, 83" x 80".
Lent by Mrs. Mary Pestana, Maui.

KOALI PEHU, (Morning Glory)
Made by Mrs. Mary R. Medinos for her daughter Mary, ca. 1910, Maui,
cotton, lavender, blue, yellow, green. Quilting: following the
pattern and small squares, 110½″ x 94½″.
Lent by Mrs. Mary Pestana, Maui.

46

LIKO LEHUA O PANA-'EWA, (Lehua Buds of Pana-'ewa)
Made by Mrs. Kamakee Paki Saffery for the present owner, 1915, Maui,
percale, red and yellow. Quilting: following the pattern, 90" x 90".
Lent by Mrs. Winnifred S. Sanborn, Maui.

47

LIHIWAI O KANAHA, (The Banks of Kanaha Stream)
Made for Mrs. Dora R. Isenberg, 1912, Kauai, cotton, pink on white.
Quilting: following the pattern, 66" x 50".
Lent by Mrs. Dora Jane Cole, Kauai.

KU'U HAE ALOHA, (My Beloved Flag)
*Made by "the women of the Mission Church" (probably Kawaiahao
Church, Honolulu) for Lorrin Andrew III, 1910. Percale, red, white,
blue, yellow. Quilting: following the pattern, 88" x 76".
Collection of Hawaiian Mission Children's Society, Oahu.*

CROWN OF INDIA
Made for Maria K. Dunn before 1913, Oahu, cotton, muslin, red on white. Quilting: following the pattern, 87" x 79".
Lent by Mrs. John Kaholokula, Maui.

50

NANI AHIAHI, (Beautiful Evening)
Made before 1918, cotton, red, white, blue.
Quilting: following the pattern and parallel lines, 80″ x 80″.
Lent by Mrs. Edward A. O'Neill, Oahu.

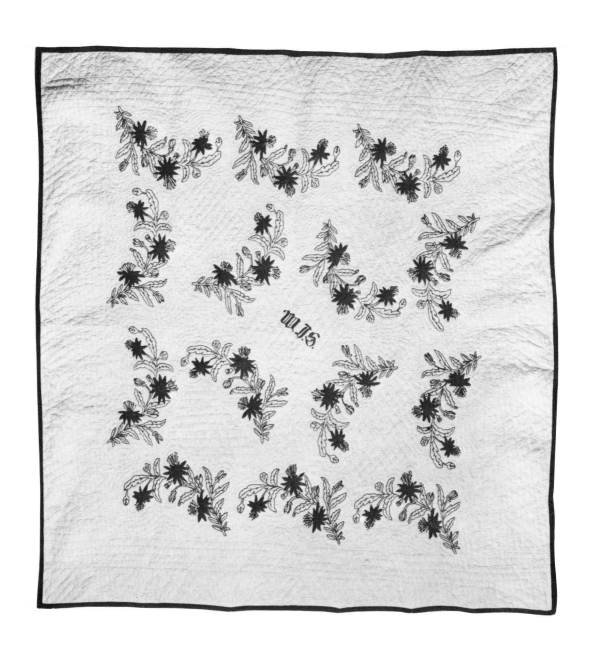

PANINI, (Prickly Pear)
Designed by Mrs. William Sanborn; made by Mrs. Kamakee Paki
Saffery, 1915, Maui, percale, red on white.
Quilting: following the pattern and squares, 78" x 78".
Lent by Mrs. Wailani S. Johansen, Maui.

KU'U HAE ALOHA, (My Beloved Flag)
Made by Mrs. Hoopii for owner, 1915, Kauai, cotton, red, white, blue.
Quilting: following the pattern, 88" x 87".
Lent by Mrs. Minerva L. Kalama, Maui.

HALA 'AI, (Pineapple)
Probably made for William F. Pogue, before 1918, Maui,
cotton, blue on white.
Quilting: following the pattern, 84" x 84".
Lent by Mrs. Edna E. Jenkins, Maui.

54

KE KAHI O KA KAIULANI, (The Comb of Kaiulani)
Made before 1918, cotton, red on white.
Quilting: parallel lines, 88½" x 84".
Collection of Honolulu Academy of Arts.

ACORN
Made before 1917, cotton, red, orange, white.
Quilting: following the pattern, 77" x 73".
Lent by Mrs. William K. McKee, Sr., Oahu.

56

NA KALAUNU, (Crowns)
Made before 1918, cotton, lavender on yellow.
Quilting: following the pattern, 82½" x 81½".
Collection of Honolulu Academy of Arts.

"IN GOD WE TRUST"
Made before 1918, cotton, red, white, blue.
Quilting: parallel lines, 87½" x 82".
Collection of Daughters of Hawaii.

KU'U HAE ALOHA, (My Beloved Flag)
Made before 1918, Hawaii, cotton, red, white, blue, yellow, green.
Quilting: parallel lines, 90" x 90".
Collection of Honolulu Academy of Arts.

COAT-OF-ARMS AND KAHILIS
Made before 1918, cotton, red, white, blue.
Quilting: following the pattern, 82½" x 78".
Collection of Daughters of Hawaii.

60

KULI PU'U, (Bent Knee)
Made before 1918, Kauai, cotton, red, white, blue.
Quilting: following the pattern, 92" x 82".
Collection of Honolulu Academy of Arts.

KU'U HAE ALOHA, (My Beloved Flag)
Made before 1918, cotton, red, white, blue.
Quilting: diagonal blocks, 90½" x 84½".
Collection of Honolulu Academy of Arts.

TITLE UNKNOWN
Made before 1918, cotton, red on white.
Quilting: following the pattern, 83" x 83".
Lent by Mrs. Minerva L. Kalama, Maui.

"IN GOD WE TRUST"
*Made for Mrs. Felix DuBois as a gift from David Nakoa, before
1918, Maui, cotton, red, white, blue, yellow.
Quilting: diagonal blocks, 78" x 78".*

Lent by Mrs. Charles F. DuBois, Maui.

NA KALAUNU ME NA ILIMA, (Crowns and Ilima)
Made before 1918, cotton, yellow on white.
Quilting: following the pattern, 96" x 84".
Lent by Mrs. Euphence Fleming Vockrodt, Maui.

KU'U HAE ALOHA, (My Beloved Flag)
Probably made for Mr. and Mrs. H. W. Rice before 1918, cotton, red,
white, blue, yellow.
Quilting: following the pattern and parallel lines, 93" x 81".
Lent by Mrs. Garfield King, Maui.

KAOMI MALIE, (Press Gently)
Made before 1918, cotton, blue on white.
Quilting: following the pattern, 85″ x 83½″.
Collection of Honolulu Academy of Arts.

KE KUMU WAINA, (Grapevine)
Made before 1918, Hawaii, calico on cotton, red on white.
Quilting: diagonal parallel lines, 84" x 84".
Collection of Honolulu Academy of Arts.

68

TITLE UNKNOWN
Probably made for Mr. and Mrs. William Richards Castle, before 1918,
cotton, yellow on red.
Quilting: following the pattern, 84½" x 82½".
Lent by Mr. and Mrs. Lester J. Will, Oahu.

LOKELANI, (Rose)
*Made by Mrs. Hattie Diamond for owner, before 1918, Maui,
cotton, blue on white.*
Quilting: following the pattern, 74" x 74".
Lent by Mrs. Minerva L. Kalama, Maui.

NA WAIOLEKA, (Violets)
Made by Mrs. Kulia Kaala Scharsch, before 1918, Kauai,
cotton, lavender on white.
Quilting: following the pattern and squares, 78" x 74".
Collection of Kauai Museum.

TITLE UNKNOWN
Made before 1918, cotton, pink on white.
Quilting: following the pattern, 87" x 76".
Collection of Kauai Museum.

NA KIHAPAI NANI LUA 'OLE O EDENA A ME ELENALE,
(The Garden of Eden and the Garden of Elenale)
Made before 1918, calico on cotton, red, yellow, pink, brown.
Quilting: following the pattern, 85" x 83½".
Collection of Honolulu Academy of Arts.

NA KALAUNU ME KA LEI MAILE, (Crowns and Maile Lei)
*Made by Mrs. Sophie Sheldon, a lady of prominence in Queen
Liliuokalani's court, before 1918, Oahu, cotton, white on red.
Quilting: following the pattern, 73½" x 66½".
Collection of Daughters of Hawaii.*

KAOMI MALIE, (Press Gently)
Made before 1918, cotton, red on white.
Quilting: following the pattern, 85" x 80".
Lent by Mrs. Raymond R. Lyons, Maui.

LOKELANI, (Rose)
Made before 1918, chambray, blue on white.
Quilting: following the pattern, 77½" x 77½".
Collection of Daughters of Hawaii.

KU'U HAE ALOHA, (My Beloved Flag)
Made before 1918, cotton, red, white, blue, yellow, brown.
Quilting: following the pattern, diagonal lines, 85½" x 83".
Collection of Honolulu Academy of Arts.

KAPA POHO, (Patchwork Quilt)
Made by Mrs. Mary K. Robinson, 1860-1870, Hawaii, various materials,
multicolored. Quilting: none; embroidery stitches, 80" x 78".

Lent by Mrs. Mary Luddington, Hawaii.